Elisabeth Luard

Vegetable Soups

D0996215

ELISABETH LUARD

Vegetable Soups

Photography by Simon Wheeler

WEIDENFELD & NICOLSON

Elisabeth Luard

Elisabeth Luard's gastronomic tastes have never been anything but cosmopolitan. A peripatetic childhood as a diplomatic daughter was followed by marriage to co-founder of *Private Eye*, Nicholas Luard. With four children to bring up, she moved to Spain and subsequently to France. In 1986 she published her first cookbook, *European Peasant Cookery*, and in 1992 she both wrote and illustrated *Flavours of Andalucia*, which won the coveted Glenfiddich Award for Food Book of the Year. Her most recent book is *Family Life – Birth, Death and the Whole Damn Thing*, an autobiography-with-recipes. She has also written two novels, *Emerald* and *Marguerite*, has a weekly column in *The Sunday Telegraph* and contributes regularly to *House & Garden* and *Country Living*.

Contents

THE BASICS

Take a short view of life.

No further than dinner or tea.

REV. SYDNEY SMITH.
ADVICE TO A YOUNG LADY IN LOW SPIRITS
(Circa 1830)

Introduction

Easy to prepare, cheap and delicious – clear uncomplicated flavours are the essence of a good soup. Innocence is all – simple dishes are at their best when the ingredients speak for themselves. A pottage, after all, is hunter-gatherer food, the most ancient culinary preparation since cavewoman first got bored of boiling bison in its skin.

No complicated stocks are necessary, although a good vegetable or chicken broth will add depth and richness of flavour. With the exception of the Chinese mushroom soup, all these recipes can be made with plain water, with perhaps a glass of wine for a little kick to the flavour, a dash of vinegar to bring out the sweetness of onion or underpin the earthy flavour of root vegetables.

The dozen I have chosen are my own family's favourites, not only because they're delicious but also because each reflects regional culinary habit. A mulligatawny tells tales of the Raj; a Jamaican pea soup captures the essence of West Indian sunshine; a Spanish gazpacho shows its aristocratic breeding in the elegance of its accompaniments.

Whether hearty meal-in-a-bowl for everyday family fare, coolly refreshing on a summer picnic, gloriously warming on a cold winter's evening, or deliciously dressed for dinner with gorgeous garnishes, there's a soup for all seasons and all occasions.

CARROT AND GINGER SOUP

SERVES 4 – 6

2 tablespoons sunflower or
   soya oil
1 onion, finely sliced
675 g/1½ lb carrots, finely sliced
2 tablespoons finely slivered
   fresh ginger
900 ml/1½ pints water
2 tablespoons ginger wine or
   1 tablespoon honey
1 tablespoon butter
salt and pepper

To garnish

a slice of fresh ginger, cut into
   matchsticks

Heat the oil gently in a heavy saucepan, add the onion and cook over a low heat for about 10 minutes, stirring regularly, until it softens – don't let it brown.

Stir in the carrots and ginger, cover and cook gently for another 10 minutes, stirring occasionally to avoid sticking.

Add the water and the ginger wine or honey, bring to the boil, then cover, turn down the heat and leave to simmer for 30 minutes or so, until the carrots are perfectly soft.

Let the soup cool for a minute or two, then add the butter and tip everything into a food processor or use a hand-held liquidizer to blend to a purée.

To serve, reheat gently and season to taste. Don't be tempted to add cream. Serve in hot bowls, scattered with a few matchsticks of ginger.

Delicious accompanied by small croque-monsieurs: cheese and ham sandwiches fried in a little butter and oil, cut into bite-sized triangles. Complete a light meal with a green salad made with mustardy leaves (always good with cheesy things) and a decadent dessert – strawberry tart or lemon meringue pie.

CHINESE MUSHROOM SOUP

SERVES 4–6

25 g/1 oz dried Chinese
mushrooms (shiitake,
wood-ears)
1 litre/1¾ pints homemade
chicken stock (page 34)
6 spring onions (white parts only
– use the green parts for the
garnish), sliced
2–3 slices of fresh ginger, cut
into matchsticks
1–2 star anise
a pinch of sugar
1 tablespoon soy sauce
1 small glass Chinese rice wine
or dry sherry or white wine

To finish

50 g/2 oz Chinese transparent
noodles (vermicelli)
6 spring onions (green parts),
finely sliced on the diagonal
a small bunch of watercress or a
handful of fresh spinach,
shredded
a dash of wine vinegar
salt
fresh coriander leaves

Put the dried mushrooms in a small bowl, cover with hot water and leave to soak and swell for 10 minutes. Drain, reserving the soaking water, and trim off the tough stalks.

Put the mushrooms into a saucepan with their soaking water (leaving behind any sandy deposit) and add the stock, spring onions, ginger, star anise, sugar, soy sauce and wine. Bring to the boil. Skim off any foam, turn down the heat, cover and simmer for 30 minutes.

Meanwhile, put the transparent noodles in a small bowl and cover with boiling water. Leave to soak for 5 minutes, then rinse in cold water (or follow the instructions on the packet).

Strain the soup into a clean bowl. Pick the mushrooms out of the strainer, slice or tear into shreds, and return them to the broth.

To serve, bring the broth back to the boil. Stir in the soaked noodles, the finely sliced spring onions, the watercress or spinach and the vinegar. Taste and add salt if necessary. Serve in small bowls, with a sprinkling of fresh coriander.

This is nice with a few small spring rolls or crispy wantons to nibble, and a few rosy radishes.

The Chinese take clear soup as a refreshment during the meal rather than as a starter, so your soup can feature in any Chinese meal – even a takeaway. As a rough rule of thumb, serve as many dishes for sharing as you have diners, plus rice. Think about the balance of the meal – something crisp, something soft, something saucy, something dry.

QUICK GAZPACHO

SERVES 4–6

300 ml/½ pint tomato juice or
vegetable juice
½ slice of white bread, roughly
torn
600 ml/1 pint cold water
1 tablespoon wine vinegar
½ green pepper, deseeded and
roughly chopped
¼ cucumber, peeled and roughly
chopped
1 thick slice of mild Spanish
onion, roughly chopped
1 garlic clove, roughly chopped
2 tablespoons olive oil
1 tablespoon sugar
a pinch of chilli powder or a dash
of Tabasco sauce
a pinch of celery salt
4 ice cubes

To garnish

1 thick slice of onion, finely
chopped
¼ cucumber, diced small
2 ripe tomatoes, diced small
½ green pepper, deseeded and
diced small
1 hard-boiled egg, chopped
(optional)
a slice of serrano or Parma ham,
diced (optional)
2 slices of bread, diced and fried
in olive oil until crisp

In a liquidizer or food processor, blend all the soup
ingredients, including the ice, until quite smooth.
Taste and adjust the seasoning – cold food needs
to be highly seasoned.

Serve in bowls you have rinsed round with ice to cool
them. Put the garnishes in separate small bowls, so each
person can choose what to sprinkle on his or her soup.
Fry the croûtons at the last minute: they should be so
hot they sizzle when they hit the soup.

*Complete the meal lightly with a classic Spanish tortilla,
or more substantially with a chicken roasted with lots of garlic
and olive oil. Finish with some fresh juicy fruit – strawberries,
peaches, grapes, melon. Gazpacho is the national dish of
Andalusia, where the natives rarely serve anything but fruit
after a meal.*

*You could make double quantities of the gazpacho and keep
half in the refrigerator to be diluted with more iced water and
served (without its garnishes) as a refreshing summer drink.
Omit the onion if you're going to keep it for more than a
couple of days, as onion ferments easily.*

Mexican avocado soup

SERVES 4–6

2 perfectly ripe avocados
½ cucumber, peeled and
  chopped
1 small green chilli, deseeded
  and chopped
1 thick slice of mild onion,
  roughly chopped
1 garlic clove, sliced
juice of 2 limes or 1 lemon
a small handful of fresh
  coriander leaves
600 ml/1 pint cold water
  (or hot chicken stock)
salt

To serve
a few coriander leaves
quartered lime or lemon
coarse salt
tortilla chips
chilled tequila (optional)

Halve the avocados, remove the stones and scoop out the flesh. Put the flesh in a liquidizer with the rest of the ingredients and blend thoroughly. Taste and adjust the seasoning, remembering that you will be handing round salt and lime quarters for people to add their own. Chill for at least 30 minutes.

Serve the chilled soup in small bowls, topping each portion with a coriander leaf. Hand the lime quarters, coarse salt and tortilla chips separately.

To make a Mexican splash, accompany with little glasses of very cold tequila, either to sip with a suck of lime and a lick of salt, or to stir directly into the delicate creamy green soup.

The Mexicans also serve this soup hot: use boiling chicken stock instead of cold water, prepare it just before you're ready to serve and don't reheat.

Complete the meal Mexican-style with a grilled fish or chicken and a fiery chilli salsa, served with refried frijoles, cooked black beans squished into a frying pan with oil and garlic and fried to crisp the base, as for a hash. Finish with fresh papaya with lime juice.

BULGARIAN MONASTERY SOUP

SERVES 4 AS A MAIN COURSE

85 g/3 oz round rice ('pudding' or risotto)
4 tablespoons corn oil
1 garlic clove, finely chopped
1 green pepper, deseeded and chopped
1 small green chilli, deseeded and chopped
1 fat leek, trimmed and finely sliced (with its green parts)
1 small lettuce, shredded
a sprig of thyme
2 bay leaves
1.2 litres/2 pints water
salt and pepper

To finish
150 ml/¼ pint thick creamy yogurt
1 egg
1 tablespoon chopped fresh parsley
1 tablespoon chopped fresh dill
pickled cucumbers

Pick over the rice and remove any small stones.

Warm the oil in a large saucepan and add the garlic, green pepper and chilli. Let the vegetables cook gently until soft but not browned. Stir the rice into the fragrant oil. When the grains turn opaque, add the sliced leek, the lettuce and the herbs, pour in the water and bring to the boil. Turn the heat down, cover loosely and simmer very gently for about 30 minutes, until the rice is tender.

To finish, remove the soup from the heat. Whisk the yogurt and egg with a ladleful of the hot soup, and stir it back into the soup. Let it stand for a minute to allow the egg to set a little. Taste and adjust the seasoning.

Serve in hot soup plates, sprinkled with parsley and dill. Accompany with pickled cucumbers and dark bread – black rye bread with caraway seeds for ethnic correctness.

This is a Bulgarian recipe, and the Bulgarians are famous not only for their yogurt, but also for being the best gardeners in eastern Europe. An apple tart or peach cobbler will complete the meal authentically.

SPANISH CHICKPEA AND PEPPER SOUP

SERVES 4 AS A MAIN COURSE

225 g/8 oz dried chickpeas,
   soaked overnight in enough
   water to cover, or 450 g/1 lb
   canned chickpeas
1 litre/1¾ pints water
2–3 garlic cloves
2 tablespoons olive oil
1 ham bone or 2–3 slices of
   bacon, chopped
1 bay leaf
½ teaspoon coriander seeds
¼ teaspoon black peppercorns,
   crushed
1 onion, roughly chopped
4 tablespoons chopped fresh
   parsley
2 tablespoons chopped fresh
   mint
1 teaspoon oregano or marjoram
   (fresh or dried)
1 large potato, sliced
a large handful of spinach,
   shredded
salt

To finish

1 red pepper, deseeded and cut
   into strips
2 tablespoons olive oil
1 garlic clove, roughly sliced
chopped fresh parsley

If using soaked dried chickpeas, drain them and put them in a saucepan with the water and bring to the boil. Skim off the foam as it rises. Stick the garlic cloves on the point of knife and hold them in a flame until the papery covering blackens at the edges. Drop the singed garlic cloves in with the chickpeas. Add the olive oil, ham bone or bacon, bay leaf, coriander, peppercorns, onion and herbs. Bring back to the boil, then turn down the heat, cover and cook for 1½–2 hours, until the chickpeas are quite soft. Keep the liquid at a rapid simmer, don't add salt, and if you need to add more water, make sure it's boiling.

If using tinned chickpeas, drain, add to the water with all the flavourings, and cook for 30 minutes.

When the chickpeas are tender and well-flavoured, remove the ham bone if using, add the sliced potato and cook until tender. Stir in the spinach and bring back to the boil. Add salt to taste.

Meanwhile, fry the strips of pepper in the olive oil with the garlic until the peppers soften and caramelize a little.

Serve the soup piping hot, with a spoonful of the peppers and their oily and garlicky juices in each serving. Sprinkle with parsley and serve with plenty of rough country bread rubbed with tomato and garlic.

A salad of Cos lettuce, chunks of cucumber, quartered hard-boiled eggs and sliced mild onion dressed with olive oil, salt and vinegar completes the meal in proper Spanish style.

BROAD BEAN AVGOLEMONO
with lovage

SERVES 4 – 6

450 g/1 lb shelled fresh broad
    beans or 225 g/8 oz dried
    broad beans (fava), soaked
    overnight and drained
1 onion, chopped
1 stalk of lovage (or fennel or
    celery), finely shredded
1 teaspoon grated lemon zest
juice of ½ lemon
2 tablespoons olive oil
1 litre/1¾ pints vegetable or
    chicken stock (page 34) or
    water
1 glass dry white wine
salt and pepper

To finish

2 small eggs
juice of ½ lemon
4 spring onions, chopped
2 tablespoons chopped fresh
    parsley
lemon quarters

Pick over the broad beans. If they are elderly or dried-out, nick out the little black 'key' and skin them. If they are young and tender include some of the young pods (de-stringed and chopped) – these have a lovely asparagus-like flavour.

Put all the soup ingredients in a large saucepan and bring to the boil. Cover and simmer for about 30 minutes (or at least 1 hour if using dried beans), until the beans are quite tender.

To finish, remove the soup from the heat and whisk the eggs with the lemon juice. Whisk a ladleful of the hot soup into the egg-and-lemon mixture and stir this back into the soup. Don't reboil the soup or it will curdle. Serve immediately, sprinkled with chopped spring onions and parsley, accompanied by quartered lemons and plenty of bread to mop up the broth.

This is the Greek method of thickening soups and sauces: avgolemono means egg-and-lemon. Begin the meal with a salad of roughly chunked tomatoes, cucumber and mild onion dressed with fresh oregano, olive oil, salt and black olives. Grilled meat can follow if you're hungry, or maybe a shoulder of lamb baked in the oven with garlic and oregano. To finish in high Hellenic style, serve baclava or thick sheep's milk yogurt with honey and nuts.

HUNGARIAN PAPRIKA SOUP

SERVES 4 AS A MAIN COURSE

3 tablespoons lard (or oil plus a
    rasher or two of bacon,
    chopped)
450 g/1 lb onions, finely sliced
salt
1 carrot, diced small
½ red pepper, deseeded and
    diced small
1 potato, diced
1 teaspoon caraway seeds
2 heaped tablespoons sweet
    paprika
1 litre/1¾ pints water
1 glass red wine
1 tablespoon tomato purée
2 bay leaves
1 teaspoon chopped marjoram
50 g/2 oz pasta bows or shells
a pinch of sugar

To finish
1 fresh red or green chilli,
    deseeded and finely chopped,
    or 1 teaspoon chilli powder
soured cream (or thick yogurt)

Heat the lard (or oil and bacon) gently in a heavy
saucepan and cook the onions until they soften and
turn golden – sprinkle with a little salt to draw the
water and speed up the process. It's this preliminary
light roasting that gives the flavour to all Hungarian
soups and stews.

Push the onions to one side and add the diced carrot,
red pepper and potato. Sprinkle with the caraway seeds
and a little more salt. Let the vegetables sizzle for a
minute or two, then stir in the paprika – it should just
soak up the oil rather than fry. Add the water, wine,
tomato purée, bay leaves and marjoram. Stir, bring to
a rolling boil, then turn down the heat. Cover loosely
and leave to simmer gently for 15 minutes, until the
vegetables soften.

Add the pasta, bring back to the boil, then turn
down the heat, cover and leave to simmer for another
12–15 minutes, until everything is tender. Taste and
adjust the seasoning.

To finish, transfer a ladleful of the hot soup to a small
bowl and stir in the finely chopped fresh chilli or chilli
powder. Hand this chilli mixer separately, along with
soured cream, so that each person can control the
pepperiness and creaminess of the soup. The colder the
day, the more welcome the chilli – an excellent source
of sniffle-defying vitamin C in winter.

*A cherry or plum-stuffed strudel will complete the meal in true
Magyar style.*

MULLIGATAWNY

SERVES 4–6

50 g/2 oz butter

1 onion, chopped

2 tablespoons curry powder
 or paste

1 small turnip, diced

1 parsnip, diced

1 carrot, diced

1 potato, diced

85 g/3 oz orange lentils
 (masoor dal)

1 litre/1¾ pints vegetable stock
 or water

salt and pepper

To garnish

chopped fresh coriander (or
 parsley and a pinch of ground
 coriander)

1 green chilli, deseeded and
 finely sliced

thick yogurt stirred with mint or
 grated cucumber

toasted grated coconut

toasted flaked almonds

chopped raw onion and apple
 dressed with lemon juice

chopped tomato spiked with a
 little chilli

chutney

poppadums

Melt the butter in a large saucepan, add the onion and fry until it is lightly caramelized. Stir in the curry powder or paste. Add the rest of the vegetables and the lentils, along with the stock or water. Bring to the boil, cover loosely, turn down the heat and simmer for 30–40 minutes, until the vegetables and lentils are perfectly tender.

Tip half the soup into a food processor or liquidizer and blend to a purée. Return to the saucepan, taste and adjust the seasoning and reheat until boiling.

Serve hot, sprinkled with coriander and a ring or two of green chilli. Serve the remaining garnishes in small bowls, to be stirred into this thick soup, or spooned on top. Accompany with any of the Indian breads: naan, paratha, chappati.

You will not need anything too sturdy after a soup like this. Maybe something from the tandoori oven – a joint of chicken or a skewerful of spiced prawns with a few crisp lettuce leaves. A coconut ice or a fresh mango will refresh the palate after all those spices.

CATALAN 'BULLIT'

SERVES 4 AS A MAIN COURSE

1 tablespoon olive oil
1 large onion, finely chopped
½ green or red pepper, deseeded
   and chopped
1 stick of celery, chopped
225 g/8 oz small new potatoes,
   scrubbed and cut into bite-
   sized pieces
1 litre/1¾ pints water
salt
1 small courgette, diced
125 g/4 oz young green beans,
   topped and tailed, or
   125 g/4 oz shelled peas
   (fresh or frozen)
a handful of spinach or Swiss
   chard, shredded

To finish

2 tablespoons olive oil
3–4 spring onions, finely sliced
4 tablespoons chopped fresh
   parsley
2 tablespoons chopped fresh
   marjoram
grated zest of 1 lemon
1 garlic clove, finely chopped
salt and pepper

To serve
aïoli (page 37)

Warm the oil in a large saucepan or casserole. Add the onion and fry gently for a few minutes. Add the chopped pepper and celery and let everything sizzle until soft but not browned. Add the potatoes, water and 1 teaspoon salt and bring to the boil.

Turn down the heat, cover and leave to simmer for 15–20 minutes. Add the courgette and beans and cook for a further 8–10 minutes; stir in the spinach a few minutes before the end of the cooking time. The potatoes should be tender and the consistency of the dish should be midway between a stew and a soup.

To finish, just before serving stir in the oil (olive oil is used here both as a seasoning and a thickening), spring onions and herbs, lemon zest and garlic. Bring back to a full boil to amalgamate the oil, then taste and add freshly ground black pepper and extra salt if necessary.

For a more substantial dish, poach eggs in the broth: drop them into hollows between the vegetables and spoon hot broth over until the whites set. Accompany with plenty of rough country bread and a bowl of aïoli.

The bullit, like a minestrone, is a meal-in-a-bowl – substantial and delicious. Follow with fruit and cheese.

PUMPKIN MINESTRONE

SERVES 4 AS A MAIN COURSE

2 tablespoons olive oil
1 large leek, finely sliced
1 stick of celery, finely sliced
1 large carrot, diced
2–3 tomatoes, skinned and
    diced
1.2 litres/2 pints boiling water
225 g/8 oz slice of pumpkin,
    peeled, deseeded and diced
1 large potato, diced
bouquet garni (thyme, parsley,
    bay leaf)
50 g/2 oz macaroni or other
    tubular pasta
1 tablespoon pesto (page 37)
salt and pepper

To finish

4 slices of day-old rough
    country bread
1 garlic clove, halved
Parmesan cheese, grated
olive oil

Heat the oil gently in a large saucepan, add the leek, celery and carrot and cook over a low heat for about 10 minutes, until softened but not browned. Add the tomatoes and then the boiling water, the diced pumpkin and potato, and bring back to the boil. Tuck in the bouquet garni and simmer for about 20 minutes or until the vegetables are nearly tender.

Stir in the pasta and cook for another 12–15 minutes, until the pasta is tender.

Stir in a generous spoonful of pesto, then taste and adjust the seasoning.

To finish, rub the bread with the garlic and place a slice in the bottom of four hot soup plates. Ladle on the soup and serve hot. Hand grated cheese and extra olive oil separately.

The country people of northern Italy, whose traditional midday meal this is, will tell you a minestrone can be made with whatever vegetables happen to be in season, and should be so thick a wooden spoon will stand up in it. A piece of fruit and perhaps an almond cake will complete the meal in northern Italian style.

JAMAICAN SPLIT PEA SOUP
with sweetcorn

SERVES 4 – 6

175 g/6 oz yellow split peas
2 tablespoons butter or ghee
   (clarified butter)
1 onion, finely chopped
1 garlic clove, sliced
1 teaspoon curry powder
   (Bols is the favourite
   brand in Jamaica)
1 teaspoon ground cumin
1 litre/1¾ pints water
salt and pepper

To finish

4 tablespoons cooked
   sweetcorn kernels
a little butter
1 fresh red chilli, deseeded
   and finely diced
chopped fresh coriander

Rinse the split peas in a sieve under cold running water. Drain well.

Melt the butter or ghee in a large saucepan and add the onion and garlic. Fry for about 2 minutes, then sprinkle in the curry powder and ground cumin and fry for a further minute or so. Add the split peas and stir well, then add the water and bring to the boil.

Turn down the heat and simmer, loosely covered, for 1½–2 hours, until the split peas are almost puréed. Give it a stir every now and again – peas may stick and burn. Watch the level of the liquid, and top up with boiling water if necessary.

To finish, heat the sweetcorn in a little butter. Taste the soup and adjust the seasoning. Serve hot in bowls, and top each serving with a spoonful of sweetcorn and a sprinkling of diced chilli and chopped coriander.

Delicious with fresh soft rolls or 'bakes': bread-dough balls flattened and fried like doughnuts. To make a meal of it, follow with something really Jamaican such as ackee and saltfish, crab patties or jerk pork. Finish with papaya with lime juice – or maybe a granita made with crushed fresh pineapple. Sunny days be with you.

The Basics

CHICKEN STOCK

MAKES 600 ml/1 PINT

½ chicken (or 1 kg/2 lb chicken
   bones – could be from the
   Sunday roast)
1 onion, not peeled but quartered
1 leek, roughly chopped
1 large carrot, roughly chopped
1 stick of celery, roughly chopped
a small bunch of parsley
2 bay leaves
6 peppercorns
6 allspice berries
½ teaspoon salt

Put the chicken (include the skin for the golden tinge
it gives to the stock) in a large saucepan with the leek,
carrot, celery and 1.5 litres /a generous 2 pints of water.
Bring to the boil and skim off any foam which rises.

Add the parsley, bay leaves, peppercorns, allspice and salt.
Turn down the heat and leave to simmer gently, loosely
covered, for about 1 hour, until you have a pale, well-
flavoured broth. Strain.

Boil the broth, uncovered, until you have about 600ml/
1 pint strong stock. Leave it to cool, freeze in cubes in
an ice-cube tray, then pop the cubes into a freezer bag.

To use, dilute to taste and bring back to the boil.
You can keep the stock in the refrigerator if you prefer
– but not for longer than a week.

Vegetable stock

MAKES ABOUT 1 LITRE/1¾ PINTS

2 tablespoons vegetable oil
2 onions, finely chopped
2 carrots, finely chopped
1 small fennel bulb with its
    leaves, chopped
2–3 sticks of celery with leaves,
    chopped
2 leeks, rinsed and sliced
finely pared zest and juice of
    1 lemon
150 ml/5fl oz water
150 ml/5fl oz dry white wine
2 star anise
1/4 teaspoon white peppercorns
1/2 teaspoon coriander seeds
1 bay leaf
salt

Warm the oil in a large saucepan, add the onions and fry until softened but not browned. Stir in the remaining vegetables and let them warm through, but do not fry them. Add the lemon zest, water and wine, stir, and bring to the boil.

Turn down the heat, cover loosely and simmer gently for 30 minutes.

Roughly crush the star anise, peppercorns and coriander and add to the pan together with the bay leaf and a little salt. Pour in 1 litre/1¾ pints water and bring back to the boil. Cover loosely and simmer for a further 20 minutes or so.

Take the pan off the heat, stir in the lemon juice and leave to infuse in a cold place – it's best if you leave it overnight. Strain and freeze in cubes in an ice-cube tray, or keep in the refrigerator for a day or two. This stock is wonderfully fragrant; dilute it if you wish.

To thicken and season soup

To thicken and season a vegetable soup, stir in a tablespoon or three of olive oil right at the end of the cooking. Bring the soup back to the boil and then remove it from the heat (or stir in a little cold water). Do this two or three times, as for a bouillabaisse, the famous Mediterranean fish soup which takes its name from this most venerable culinary process.

The oil droplets distribute themselves throughout the broth, producing a very light thickening with no trace of oiliness.

Choose a cold-pressed virgin olive oil – Greek for value – well worth the extra money since a little goes a long way. Virgin olive oil is the pure juice of the fruit which, having been neither subjected to heat nor chemically rectified, has a natural pepperiness which seasons and enhances without overpowering the delicate flavour of fresh vegetables.

It's best to keep the bottle in the refrigerator once it's been opened, and don't worry if it appears cloudy when it's cold – it'll liquefy again at room temperature.

Pesto

MAKES ABOUT 300 ML/½ PINT

6 garlic cloves, peeled
300 ml/½ pint fresh basil leaves
50 g/2 oz pine kernels, toasted
50 g/2 oz Pecorino or Parmesan
    cheese, grated
1 teaspoon salt
about 150 ml/5fl oz olive oil

Put the garlic, basil, pine kernels, grated cheese, salt
and a little less than 150 ml/5fl oz of the oil into
a food processor and process to a purée. With the
motor running, trickle in enough extra oil (as if for
a mayonnaise) to make a thick sauce.

Aïoli

SERVES 4 – 6

1 garlic clove, peeled and
    pounded to a paste
1 egg yolk
about 150 ml/5fl oz olive oil
1 tablespoon wine vinegar
salt

Make sure all the ingredients are at room temperature.
Put the crushed garlic and egg yolk in a deep plate and
work together with a fork. Very slowly trickle in the oil,
drop by drop at first, beating steadily with the fork.
As the sauce thickens, so you can increase the trickle –
eventually the yolk should accept all the oil. If the aïoli
looks as if it might be about to separate, fork furiously
at one corner until it becomes smooth and thick again,
and then work in the rest. Finish with vinegar and salt
to taste.

Classic Cooking

STARTERS
Jean Christophe Novelli Chef/patron of Maison Novelli, which opened in London to great acclaim in 1996. He previously worked at the Four Seasons restaurant, London.

VEGETABLE SOUPS
Elisabeth Luard Cookery writer for the *Sunday Telegraph Magazine* and author of *European Peasant Food* and *European Festival Food*, which won a Glenfiddich Award.

GOURMET SALADS
Sonia Stevenson The first woman chef in the UK to be awarded a Michelin star, at the Horn of Plenty in Devon. Author of *The Magic of Saucery* and *Fresh Ways with Fish*.

FISH AND SHELLFISH
Gordon Ramsay Chef/proprietor of one of London's most popular restaurants, Aubergine, recently awarded its second Michelin star. He is the author of *A Passion for Flavour*.

CHICKEN, DUCK AND GAME
Nick Nairn Chef/patron of Braeval restaurant near Aberfoyle in Scotland, whose BBC-TV series *Wild Harvest* was last summer's most successful cookery series, accompanied by a book.

LIVERS, SWEETBREADS AND KIDNEYS
Simon Hopkinson Former chef/patron at London's Bibendum restaurant, columnist and author of *Roast Chicken and Other Stories* and the forthcoming *The Prawn Cocktail Years*.

VEGETARIAN
Rosamond Richardson Author of several vegetarian titles, including *The Great Green Gourmet* and *Food from Green Places*. She has also appeared on television.

PASTA
Joy Davies One of the creators of *BBC Good Food Magazine*, she has been food editor of *She, Woman* and *Options* and written for the *Guardian, Daily Telegraph* and *Harpers & Queen*.

CHEESE DISHES
Rose Elliot The UK's most successful vegetarian cookery writer and author of many books, including *Not Just a Load of Old Lentils* and *The Classic Vegetarian Cookbook*.

POTATO DISHES
Patrick McDonald Author of the forthcoming *Simply Good Food* and Harvey Nichols' food consultant.

BISTRO COOKING
Anne Willan Founder and director of La Varenne Cookery School in Burgundy and West Virginia. Author of many books and a specialist in French cuisine.

ITALIAN COOKING
Anna Del Conte is the author of *The Classic Food of Northern Italy* (chosen as the 1996 Guild of Food Writers Book of the Year) and *The Gastronomy of Italy*. She has appeared on BBC-TV's *Masterchef*.

Vietnamese Cooking
Nicole Routhier One of the United States' most popular cookery writers, her books include *Cooking Under Wraps*, *Nicole Routhier's Fruit Cookbook* and the award-winning *The Foods of Vietnam*.

Malaysian Cooking
Jill Dupleix One of Australia's best known cookery writers, with columns in the *Sydney Morning Herald* and *Elle*. Author of *New Food*, *Allegro al dente* and the Master Chefs *Pacific*.

Peking Cuisine
Helen Chen Learned to cook traditional Peking dishes from her mother, Joyce Chen, the grande dame of Chinese cooking in the United States. The author of *Chinese Home Cooking*.

Stir Fries
Kay Fairfax Author of several books, including *100 Great Stir-fries*, *Homemade* and *The Australian Christmas Book*.

Noodles
Terry Durack Australia's most widely read restaurant critic and co-editor of the *Sydney Morning Herald Good Food Guide*. He is the author of *YUM!*, a book of stories and recipes.

North Indian Curries
Pat Chapman Started the Curry Club in 1982. Appears regularly on television and radio and is the author of eighteen books, the latest being *The Thai Restaurant Cookbook*.

Barbecues and Grills
Brian Turner Chef/patron of Turner's in Knightsbridge and one of Britain's most popular food broadcasters; he appears frequently on *Ready Steady Cook*, *Food and Drink* and many other television programmes.

Summer and Winter Casseroles
Anton Edelmann Maître Chef des Cuisines at the Savoy Hotel, London, and author of six books. He appears regularly on BBC-TV's *Masterchef*.

Traditional Puddings
Tessa Bramley Chef/patron of the acclaimed Old Vicarage restaurant in Ridgeway, Derbyshire. Author of *The Instinctive Cook*, and a regular presenter on a new Channel 4 daytime series *Here's One I Made Earlier*.

Decorated Cakes
Jane Asher Author of several cookery books and a novel. She has also appeared in her own television series, *Jane Asher's Christmas* (1995).

Favourite Cakes
Mary Berry One of Britain's leading cookery writers, her numerous books include *Mary Berry's Ultimate Cake Book*. She has made many television and radio appearances and is a regular contributor to cookery magazines.

Photographs © Simon Wheeler 1997

First published in 1997 by
George Weidenfeld & Nicolson
The Orion Publishing Group
Orion House
5 Upper St Martin's Lane
London WC2H 9EA

British Library Cataloguing-in-Publication data
A catalogue record for this book is available from the
British Library

ISBN 0 297 82286 1

Designed by Lucy Holmes
Edited by Maggie Ramsay
Food styling by Joy Davies
Typeset by Tiger Typeset